VIETNAM
the people

Bobbie Kalman

TOWER HAMLETS COLLEGE
Learning Centre
Poplar High Street
LONDON
E14 0AF

A Bobbie Kalman Book

The Lands, Peoples, and Cultures Series

Crabtree Publishing Company

www.crabtreebooks.com

The Lands, Peoples, and Cultures Series

Created by Bobbie Kalman

For Andrea,
who loved visiting Vietnam

Written by
Bobbie Kalman

Coordinating editor
Ellen Rodger

Editor
Jane Lewis

Contributing editors
Kate Calder
P.A. Finlay
Carrie Gleason

Editors/first edition
Lisa Gunby
David Schimpky

Production coordinator
Rose Gowsell

Design and production
Text Etc.

Separations and film
Quadratone Graphics Ltd.

Printer
Worzalla Publishing Company

Consultants
Nancy Tingley, Wattis Curator of Southeast Asian Art, Asian Art Museum of San Francisco; Susannah Cameron; Michelle Raftus

Special thanks to
Marc Crabtree, who, during a recent assignment in Vietnam, took photographs that gave an accurate portrayal of modern Vietnam; Lance Woodruff

Photographs
Jeanette Andrews-Bertheau: p. 24; Gerald Brimacombe/International Stock: p. 4; Samantha Brown: p. 3, 5, 15 (top), 16 (bottom), 25, 27, 29, 30 (top); Patrick Burrows: p. 11 (bottom); CIDA Photo/Cindy Andrew: p. 13 (bottom); CP Picture Archive (Richard Vogel): p. 1; Marc Crabtree: cover, p. 7 (bottom), 8 (bottom), 9 (top left & top right), 12 (both), 13 (top), 15 (bottom), 16 (top), 21 (top), 23 (both), 28 (all); Jean-Leo Dugast/Panos Pictures: p. 22 (bottom); Nic Dunlop/Panos Pictures: p. 7 (top); David R. Frazier/Photo Researchers: p. 18; Margot Granitsas/Photo Researchers: p. 21 (bottom); Hulton Archive/Getty Images: p. 6; Wolfgang Kaehler: p. 8 (top), 10, 14, 17 (both), 22 (top), 28; Noboru Komine/Photo Researchers: p. 19; Steve Raymer/ Corbis/Magmaphoto: p. 31 (bottom); Paul Stepan-Vierow/Photo Researchers: p. 20, 26; Alison Wright/Photo Researchers: p. 9 (bottom), 11 (top)

Every effort has been made to obtain the appropriate credit and full copyright clearance for all images in this book. Any oversights, despite Crabtree's greatest precautions, will be corrected in future editions.

Illustrations
Scott Mooney: icons
David Wysotski, Allure Illustrations: back cover

Cover: Bicycles are a popular way for people to get from place to place in Vietnam, even when it rains!

Title page: A young girl is dressed in traditional Vietnamese clothing and takes part in a parade in Hanoi, Vietnam's capital city.

Icon: The *non-la* hat protects farmers from the sun.

Back cover: Water buffalo are used in farming.

Published by
Crabtree Publishing Company

PMB 16A,
350 Fifth Avenue
Suite 3308
New York
N.Y. 10118

612 Welland Avenue
St. Catharines
Ontario, Canada
L2M 5V6

73 Lime Walk
Headington
Oxford OX3 7AD
United Kingdom

Cataloging in Publication Data
Kalman, Bobbie, 1947-
  Vietnam. The people / Bobbie Kalman.-- Rev. ed.
    p. cm. -- (The Lands, peoples, and cultures series)
  Includes index.
  Summary: Examines aspects of Vietnamese society, including family ties, types of homes, city and village life, clothing, language, employment, ethnic minorities, and leisure activities.
  ISBN 0-7787-9356-7 (RLB) -- ISBN 0-7787-9724-4 (pbk.)
  1. Vietnam--Social life and customs--Juvenile literature. [1. Vietnam--Social life and customs.] I. Title. II. Series.
  DS556.42 .K35 2002
  959.7--dc21
                                          2001047106
                                          LC

Contents

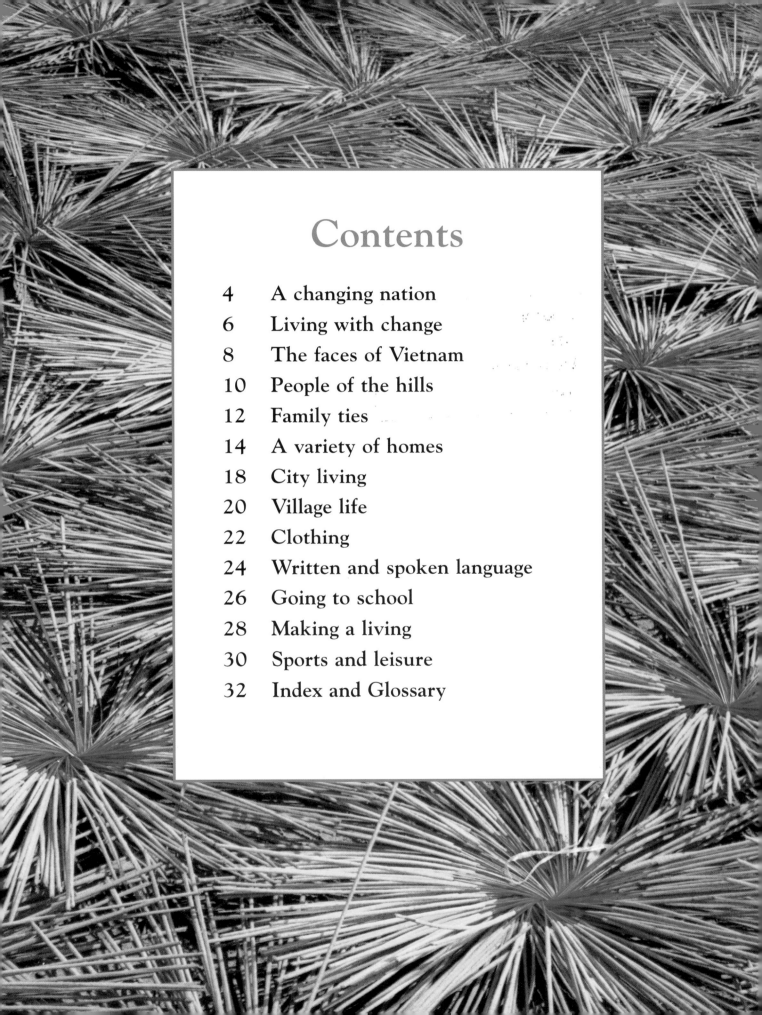

A changing nation

The Vietnamese, who number over 78 million, are an ancient people with a history of many hardships and struggles. Throughout history, they have battled for independence. The Vietnamese have been ruled by the Chinese, the French, and briefly by the Japanese. Today, they are working hard to bring more wealth and opportunity to their growing population.

Vietnam's beginnings

More than 4000 years ago, a group of people known as the Viets lived in the northern regions of what is now Vietnam. About 2000 years ago, China conquered the country. The Viet people took on many Chinese customs, however, they fought hard to keep their own nation and **culture**. In the eleventh century, Vietnam freed itself from Chinese rule. For 800 years, the Vietnamese expanded their country into the South.

They conquered different ethnic groups who became part of Vietnam. Two of these groups were the Chams in central Vietnam and the Khmer peoples in the south.

French colonization

During the 1800s, France took over Vietnam and claimed it as a French **colony**. Cambodia and Laos were also under French rule. This area was known as French Indochina. French rule was harsh and devastating to Vietnam and its people. The French government introduced high taxes and a system of forced labor. They took the valuable natural resources of the country and forced the Vietnamese to work for very little pay. There was widespread poverty, and farmers lost their land. Vietnamese people were not allowed to hold important positions, but were instead given menial jobs under the French leaders.

Rebellion against foreign control

The Vietnamese rebelled against French rule. An anti-French leader, Ho Chi Minh, gained support from the Vietnamese people. Ho Chi Minh was the leader of the Vietnamese Communist Party. Communists believe that all property and businesses should be owned by the government, and that wealth and goods should be divided equally among the country's citizens. The Vietnamese fought against the French for eight years. In 1945, France lost control of the northern half of Vietnam, which then came under communist rule. North Vietnam wanted to reunite with the south.

The Vietnam War

In the 1960s and 1970s, the Vietnam War was fought between the north and the south. For eleven years the United States was involved in the war, trying to prevent South Vietnam from being taken over by the north. The United States supported the south because they did not want the communists to gain power. The war finally came to an end in 1975. The southern city of Saigon (now called Ho Chi Minh City) was taken over by North Vietnam's communist army and the country was reunified as a communist nation.

More problems

Since the Vietnam War, the Khmer Rouge army in neighboring Cambodia, and Vietnam had been caught up in border attacks. In 1978, Vietnam invaded Cambodia. For many more years, Vietnam continued to battle with Cambodia. Thousands of people were killed or injured. A formal peace treaty was finally signed in 1991, ending the Vietnamese army's involvement in Cambodia.

(above) Although the country is peaceful today, the Vietnamese people have lived under the shadow of war for many years.

(opposite page) A statue of communist leader Ho Chi Minh stands in front of the French-built Town Hall in Ho Chi Minh City.

Living with change

People in both the north and south of Vietnam suffered from the terrible effects of the wars. Millions of people were killed, injured, or left homeless. Families were separated and at least a million people were forced to flee the country.

Effects of war

When the Vietnam War ended in 1975, the country was devastated. Roads, buildings, and bridges were destroyed. Fields were full of **land mines** that injured or killed people who walked over them. The countryside had been poisoned by chemicals during the war. Vietnam's economy was failing, and hunger was widespread.

Re-education camps

The communist government seized private property and businesses in the south. Thousands of people were sent to the countryside to work on government controlled farms. People such as religious leaders, teachers, and political leaders from the former South Vietnam were treated very badly. They were not allowed to practice their beliefs and were sent to labor camps to be "re-educated" under the communist regime.

The boat people

Hundreds of thousands of people left Vietnam because of the severe poverty and the lack of safety and health care. Most left by boat. These refugees became known as the "boat people." Attempting to escape by boat was difficult and dangerous. Refugees could take few belongings with them. Many boats were unsafe or overloaded with people, and sank before they reached a destination. Many people drowned, or died of starvation or disease.

(below) Boat people who survived the dangerous voyage landed in neighboring countries, such as Hong Kong, Thailand, Malaysia, Indonesia, Japan, and the Philippines.

New growth

The economy made a gradual recovery after a policy of reform called *doi moi* was introduced in 1986. *Doi moi* means "new thinking." Vietnamese people were given more freedom to run their own businesses and farms. Vietnam's relationship with foreign countries slowly improved, and more visitors came to the country. Strong cultural influences from other Asian countries, Europe, and North America caused some Vietnamese people to worry that their **traditional** lifestyles and customs were disappearing. Other people felt that change was necessary if their country was to become a modern nation.

Vietnam at peace

Today, Vietnam is a peaceful country. Although there is still poverty, there is less hunger. There are not enough jobs to go around, but almost everyone can read and write. The government controls many aspects of life, but more people are able to own businesses, work their own farms, and travel.

(above) Fast food restaurants owned by foreign companies are a sign of new economic freedom in Vietnam.

(below) Workers pave a city street. There was a great deal of rebuilding in Vietnam as the country recovered from the damage caused by war.

The faces of Vietnam

Close to 90 percent of Vietnam's people are ethnic Vietnamese. Their **ancestors** were the original inhabitants of the Red River Delta who settled in the north long ago. As centuries passed and these ancestors expanded their territory to the south, they pushed many other ethnic groups into remote hill and mountain regions. Today, the ethnic Vietnamese have the strongest influence on culture and government.

Ethnic minorities

Almost 60 other groups of peoples live in Vietnam. These groups are known as **ethnic minorities**. Throughout the years, the minorities have struggled to keep their own languages and traditions. Some of these groups are the Hoa, Hmong, Thai, Dao, Khmer, and Cham. Most of these groups can be found in the hills and **rural** regions of Vietnam.

The Hoa

Vietnam's largest ethnic minority is a group of Chinese descendants known as Hoa. They make up three percent of the population. The Hoa have lived in Vietnam for many **generations** yet they have maintained their distinct cultural Chinese identity. After the communist government took over Vietnam in 1975, many Hoa fled from Vietnam. Most remaining Hoa people live in Vietnam's cities. Many live in the Cholon district of Ho Chi Minh City.

(above) **This priest believes in Cao Dai,** *a modern* **faith based in southern Vietnam.**

(left) **This woman is ethnic Vietnamese.**

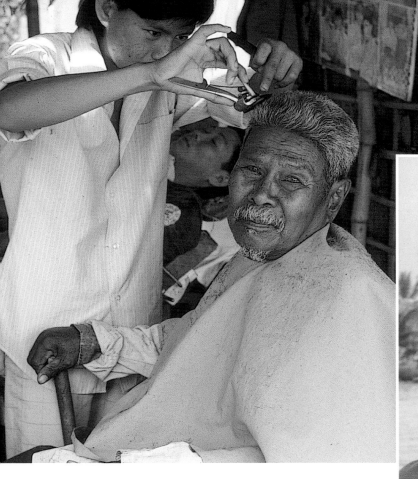

(left) There are about 450,000 Cham people in Vietnam today. They live in regions around the Mekong delta in the south.

The Chams

The Chams are an ethnic group believed to have settled in central Vietnam from Malaysia centuries ago. These people once ruled an area called the kingdom of Champa, which prospered from the 2nd to the 15th centuries. Cham culture, language, and religious beliefs were strongly influenced by traders from India. By the 18th century, all of the Champa Kingdom had been taken over by the Vietnamese.

(above) This man is an Amerasian. His mother is Vietnamese and his father is an African American who fought in the Vietnam War.

The Khmers

The Khmers are an ethnic Cambodian group. Between the 9th and 13th centuries, the Khmer Empire controlled Cambodia, Laos, Thailand, and part of Vietnam. Today, there are around 700,000 Khmer people in Vietnam, mainly living as farmers in the southern regions of the country. Almost 90 percent of Khmers are **Buddhists**.

(right) This woman belongs to the Muong hill tribe of northern Vietnam.

 # People of the hills

The remote, hilly regions of north and central Vietnam are home to over 30 different tribes. Some have lived in Vietnam for thousands of years. These people are called *Montagnards*, a French word meaning "highlanders." The hill people make up about ten percent of Vietnam's total population. The greatest number live in the northwest, near the borders of Laos and China.

The tribes

Each hill tribe has its own language, religious beliefs, and dress. The Thai tribe are known for their skillful textile weaving. The Hmong are one of the largest groups of hill people and live high in the mountains. They grow their hair long and tie it up in a giant knot. The women of the Dao tribe wear brightly colored clothing decorated with silver beads and coins. Tribes in central and south Vietnam include the Mnong, Ba Na, and Sedang. Northern tribes include the Tay, Dao, Jarai, Nung, Thai, and Muong.

Mountain life

In many tribes, the villagers live in longhouses that are shared by several families. They grow their own food, hunt, and weave their own material for clothing. Many grow crops such as rice and travel throughout the hills in order to hunt for food. Most hill people live a traditional, simple life far removed from the rest of Vietnamese society. Some, however, have adopted modern conveniences such as electricity, running water, and Western clothing styles.

(above) The people of the Ba Na hill tribe live near the coast in south-central Vietnam. The Ba Na are known for their elaborate wood carvings.

Slash and burn

Some hill peoples are nomadic, which means that they travel from place to place. Most groups stay in one area, growing rice and other crops to sell. The hill tribes often practice slash-and-burn agriculture. When they need land for crops, they cut down, or slash, all the trees and bushes in an area and burn them. The ashes from the fire add nutrients to the soil and help the rice crops grow. After a few years, however, the nutrients in the soil are all used up. The farmers then slash and burn a new area. Today, it is difficult to find new land to clear because many areas have already been farmed. Scientists are helping hill tribes develop farming methods that are less harmful to Vietnam's forests.

(right) The Muong hill tribe of northern Vietnam are known for their music, poetry, and songs.

Fighting for survival

The hill tribes have experienced terrible hardships during Vietnam's many political changes. Many were forced from their traditional homes by other peoples, such as the French, who wanted their land. Some governments tried to kill the hill peoples or change their way of life. During the wars, hill peoples were forced to fight, and their villages were attacked. Today, they strive to maintain their communities and preserve their traditions.

(left) A Nung girl looks after her younger sister. The Nung people live in the northern mountain regions of Vietnam.

Family ties

Family is at the heart of Vietnamese life. Family members give one another comfort and security. Beliefs about the importance of family are rooted in the lessons of an ancient Chinese teacher named Confucius. According to Confucius, the older people get, the wiser they get. He said that children should respect and obey adults. In turn, parents and grandparents have a duty to care for their children and raise them to be good people. Showing respect for others is evident in the Vietnamese language. There are many different ways of addressing another person, based on his or her age and gender. Using the proper form of address is a sign of respect.

(right) This man looks after his granddaughter while her mother and father are at work.

(below) Family members of all ages enjoy spending time together.

Extended families

A Vietnamese family is thought of as more than just parents and children. Grandparents, aunts, uncles, and cousins make up an extended family. Grown children often share their homes with their parents or live close by. Family members help each other in their day-to-day life. Grandparents look after the children while parents are at work and older children help by babysitting their younger brothers and sisters.

Sharing the good and bad

All members of a family share in one another's failures and successes. If a child misbehaves, the whole family is embarrassed. Young adults are expected to follow the wishes of their elders when choosing a career or a husband or wife. If they do not obey, they may be **disowned** by the family. A disowned child is ignored by relatives. If a child is successful in life, then the family shares the honor. Older generations take great pride in the accomplishments of children.

A child's life

Most Vietnamese children have few toys. They spend their free time with their family or playing with friends. Children usually start school at the age of six. They are respectful of their teachers and are eager to do well. Besides spending many hours studying for school, children take on other responsibilities at a young age. Girls help in the kitchen, wash clothes, and clean the house. Boys who live in rural areas help by looking after the animals, fetching water, and helping with the farming or fishing.

New ways for young people

Many young people, especially in the cities, are influenced by foreign fashions and ideas. They listen to the latest music from Europe and North America and wear Western clothing. In some cases, these changes worry their parents. They would prefer that their children follow the old ways and wear traditional Vietnamese clothing and hairstyles.

(right) Family shrines are colorfully decorated to honor the spirit of a dead relative.

A family forever

Even after relatives die, they remain an important part of the family. Vietnamese homes have a small **shrine** where photographs of dead relatives are displayed. Offerings of food or **incense** are made on special occasions to honor the spirits of ancestors. Some families also have spirit houses outside their homes. A spirit house is built when someone dies in the family's home. The spirit of the dead person is believed to live in this special house.

(below) Children take on responsibilities at a young age. Young boys who look after the water buffalo are called "buffalo boys."

A variety of homes

Families build homes to suit different landscapes and **climates**. In the north, small, cozy houses built of stone protect people from the cold winters. Many city homes are made of brick and have tile roofs. In the warmer south, homes are larger and are constructed of **bamboo** and wood with straw roofs. They have open windows that let cool breezes blow through.

Country living

Most houses in the southern countryside are simple, with dirt floors and no running water. Villages have a well that families share, or water is carried up from a nearby stream. Few people have electricity—lanterns light their homes at night. Homes are kept clean, and people always take their shoes off before entering. A typical village house is likely to have one large room, divided by curtains. There is very little furniture. Family members may sleep on two large beds with mattresses woven from palm leaves. Kitchens are separate from the main house and are used only for cooking. Pigs are often kept in pens next to the cooking area and chickens wander wherever they please.

(below) Homes in southern Vietnam are suited to the warm climate of that region.

(opposite page, top) This young person is having a bath at the back of his houseboat. His family and many others live on boats on the river.

(opposite page, bottom) Crowded apartment buildings are common in large cities such as Hanoi and Ho Chi Minh City.

Houses on water

Parts of Vietnam, such as the area around the great Mekong River, are crisscrossed by rivers and canals. Many people in these areas live in houseboats on the water. Fish **hatcheries** are often kept along the shores, but some fish farmers keep their hatchery below their boat. They can feed the catfish through a trap door in the bottom of the boat.

City homes

Most housing in the city is apartment buildings. Many of these buildings were cheaply constructed and are now in poor condition. Most apartments have two or three rooms, a small kitchen, and a bathroom. Often, three generations of a family live together in one apartment. Some families have a balcony or share a courtyard with others for drying laundry. Like many country houses, city homes have very little furniture. At mealtime, families sit together on the floor around a low table, and share stories about their day.

Houses on stilts

Heavy rains in the summer often cause flooding, so houses near rivers or in low-lying areas are built on stilts. Although flood waters might surround a home, stilts keep it high and dry. To support a whole house, stilts must be made from sturdy poles. People use stairs or a ladder to climb into their home.

Super stilts

Stilts have other uses as well. They allow strong winds to blow under and around the home, causing less damage. Raising a house on stilts also helps keep out snakes and wild animals, which prowl along the ground. During dry, hot seasons, work such as weaving can be done in the cool shade beneath the house. Livestock such as chickens, pigs, and water buffalo are also sheltered under the house.

(above) Many village homes have little furniture. At mealtimes, families gather together and eat on the floor.

(above) Homes near a river are often built on stilts for protection from high waters.

Mountain homes

Mountain villages are usually made up of several longhouses. Some of the long, narrow houses are large enough for several families—as many as 30 to 40 people. If more room is needed, the house is made longer by building onto one end. Visitors are invited to have tea in a common room in the center of the longhouse. They sit on mats made of palm leaves. A hearth, built in the house's center, provides heat and a place for cooking. A hole, built into the roof, lets in light and allows smoke to escape.

Mountain homes are built with a wooden frame covered by palm branches, sugar-cane leaves, and sometimes planks of wood. Some homes are surrounded by a trench to keep out wild animals. Palm trees grow around the houses and provide protection from the effects of storms.

(above) Some mountain homes are also built on stilts. The stilts provide a shady area for people and livestock during hot days.

(below) The Muong people of northern Vietnam live in longhouses. Nearby vegetable gardens provide food for the families of the village.

City living

Vietnamese cities are overcrowded. Everyday more people move from the country to find jobs in the city. Ho Chi Minh City is Vietnam's largest city with almost five million people. Hanoi, Vietnam's capital city, and Haiphong are also large cities.

In the neighborhood

Most city dwellers live in crowded apartment buildings. People tend to live close to the place they work or the school they attend. Many shopkeepers have apartments attached to their shop. They can go to work or school and shop at a local outdoor market all within the same neighborhood. Some people cannot afford to rent an apartment. These people build small shacks in poor areas outside the city. Others remain homeless and live on the streets.

Busy streets

City streets are crowded with merchants selling their wares or offering a variety of services, from pulling teeth to cutting hair. Music blares from restaurants, cafés, and karaoke bars. In the evening, music and television can also be heard from people's apartments.

A city day

The market opens early in the morning, often at six a.m. Farmers unpack their produce, salespeople set up their displays, and cooks prepare food to sell to people on their way to work. By six thirty, the streets are full of people as they hurry to school and work. Shops and businesses open at seven or eight o'clock. Between twelve noon and one thirty, people stop working and break for lunch. Most businesses close for the day at four or five o'clock, but the work day does not end for city dwellers. Many have part-time jobs in the evening to make ends meet.

(opposite page) Almost anything—fruits, flowers, vegetables, clothing, medicine, and electronics— can be found at the market. Live pigs, ducks, chickens, dogs, and snakes add to the happy confusion. People stop to buy snacks while they shop. They can even have their shoes shined, get their fortune told, or stop to get a bicycle tire fixed.

(below) Horns, bells, and music fill the air in a city. People driving cars, motorcycles, and mopeds honk their horns as they speed through the streets.

Village life

Village life in Vietnam includes a lot of hard work. Most people who live in villages are farmers or fishers. Fields have to be plowed and crops have to be planted and harvested. Most farming is done by hand using tools and simple machines pulled by water buffalo.

Working together

People in a village work together to make a living. The men perform heavy, difficult work such as plowing the fields, building homes, and digging canals. Women tend to the fields for several hours a day and also look after the household. Children help their families with chores and look after their younger brothers and sisters.

Harvest break

Schools in villages schedule long vacations for harvest time. Students spend their holiday helping on the farm. Children who work on the family farm often cannot continue their education beyond primary school.

(above) This farming family is hard at work. Their rural home is in the Mekong Delta, just south of Ho Chi Minh City in southern Vietnam. The Mekong Delta is a rich agricultural region. Rice is the primary crop, but sugar cane, coconuts, and tropical fruits such as bananas, lychees, mangos, and papayas are also grown.

Few modern conveniences

Smaller villages do not have electricity, central heat, or running water, especially if they are located far away from cities. Some villages have diesel-powered generators that provide power and many families light their homes at night with kerosene lamps. Larger villages often have a few stores, restaurants, and a barber shop.

Life on the river

Some villages are situated beside rivers. Rivers that run through Vietnam's countryside are used as highways in which vessels travel carrying goods, from coconuts to pigs, to be sold at a market. Many families who live along the river banks operate fish farms. A section of the river is fenced off and fish such as catfish and snakehead are bred and raised.

(above) Several tributaries and canals crisscross the Mekong River Delta. Often crowded with boats, these waterways are important transportation routes.

(below) Rivers provide food, transportation, and a place to bathe and do laundry for the people who live nearby.

Clothing

Today, more Vietnamese are dressing in western-style clothing. Young people wear jeans and t-shirts, women wear dresses, and business people wear suits. Traditional Vietnamese clothing is still worn, but mostly in villages and during festivals.

The *ao dai*

In the past, both men and women wore the *ao dai*. Today, it is worn mostly by women. An *ao dai* is a long blouse that resembles a dress. It has long sleeves, a short collar, and slits up the sides. It is worn over baggy pants. *Ao dais* are usually white or black, but some are brightly colored. They are often made of light material such as cotton or silk.

(right) Today, many Vietnamese young people wear western-style clothing. Blue jeans, baseball hats, and t-shirts are a popular fashion adopted from North America.

Keeping feet dry

When shoes and boots get wet, they trap moisture, which can lead to foot infections. Since Vietnam receives heavy rain showers during the summer, most people wear sandals. Feet can dry quickly in these open shoes.

Clothes in the north

In northern Vietnam, where the weather is cooler, people dress in warm clothing. The black or dark blue fabric of the hill tribes is often decorated with beautiful embroidery. Silver jewelry, beads, and pompoms are special adornments. Sometimes clothes are decorated with old coins.

(below) Winters get chilly in the northern highland regions of Vietnam. Hill tribes living in that area must dress warmly in the wintertime. This northern hill tribe woman wears a brightly colored scarf over her dark blue clothing.

Protection from the sun

The cone-shaped hats worn by farm workers are a common sight throughout Vietnam. These hats, called *non la*, are made of woven palm leaves. *Non la* are worn to protect the face and neck from the hot tropical sun. In Vietnam, it is fashionable for women to have pale skin, so some women carry umbrellas and wear long gloves up to their elbows to avoid getting suntanned.

(above) One traditional item of clothing that is still worn by people everywhere in Vietnam is the non la *hat.* Non la *hats provide shade from the sun in Vietnam's hot climate.*

(opposite page, bottom) The traditional ao dai *is a comfortable garment still worn by many women in Vietnam today.*

Written and spoken language

Vietnamese is spoken by nearly 90 percent of the population. This ancient language has developed over many centuries and shares its roots with Chinese, Cambodian, and Thai languages. Other languages spoken in Vietnam are French, Chinese, and English. The hill peoples of Vietnam speak their own languages as well.

Syllables and tones

The Vietnamese language is monosyllabic. That means it is made up of words that have only one syllable, such as *ho*, which means cough, or *kern*, which means ice cream. The language is also tonal—the meaning of a word depends on the tone of the voice. The **dialect** spoken in the north uses six tones, and the southern dialect has five tones. The tones make the Vietnamese language sound a little like singing. A word might have a high, low, middle, rising, heavy, or flat tone.

Watch your tone

The letters *ma* are a good example of how tone changes the meaning of a word. If *ma* is said using a high voice, it means mother, but if it is said with a low voice, it means rice plant. If *ma* is said with a rising tone, it means clever, but when said with a flat tone, it means ghost. Obviously, it is easy for someone learning Vietnamese to make a mistake and ask a funny question such as "Where is your ghost?" instead of "Where is your mother?" To complicate matters even more, accents differ from the north to the south of the country.

Writing it down

In the past, only the most educated people could read and write. For centuries, scholars wrote in the Chinese language. Vietnamese was only a spoken language. Then, educated people began to use the Chinese symbols to write down Vietnamese words. Each symbol represents one word. This writing system, called *chu nom*, is still used for ceremonies and traditional greetings.

A new way of writing

In the 1600s, a French **missionary** invented *quoc ngu*, a new way of writing the Vietnamese language. This writing system is based on letters and their sounds. It uses the same letters that most European languages use—the Latin alphabet. Small signs are added above or beside the letters to mark their tone. The *quoc ngu* system became very popular and is the common writing system used today.

(above) In recent decades, the government has made literacy a priority. Now 90 percent of Vietnamese people can read and write.

Literature

Poetry, fables, proverbs, and books have been written by the Vietnamese for hundreds of years. Many ancient poems were about Buddhist philosophies. Later, scholars wrote about geography, medicine, and dynasties. Doan Thi Diem is a famous historic writer. In the 1700s, she wrote a book called *New Collection of Wonderful Stories* which is a well-known book of legends. Poetry is also very popular in Vietnam. The musical sound of the Vietnamese language makes poetry beautiful to listen to. The *Tale of Kieu*, one of Vietnam's most famous poems, is a book that was written in the early 1800s by Nguyen Du. It is actually a long poem that has over 3,000 verses! The *Tale of Kieu* is known as Vietnam's national poem.

A modern writer

Duong Thu Huong is one of the best-known modern Vietnamese authors. One of her books, *Paradise of the Blind,* was the first Vietnamese book to be published in the United States. Many of Duong Thu Huong's writings criticize the government of Vietnam. Her books are now banned in Vietnam, but they are popular in many other countries around the world.

You can speak Vietnamese!

How would you like to speak Vietnamese? It is not that difficult! You can start by learning the words in the dictionary below.

A beginner's dictionary

bạn—friend	nam—south
ca—sing	nón—hat
cám ơn—thank you	sách—book
chào—hello	sinh viên—student
chó—dog	tạm biêt—goodbye
con gái—girl	tên—name
con trai—boy	vâng—yes
hoa—flower	nguời viêt—people
kern—ice cream	voi—elephant
mèo—cat	má—mother

(left) Most newspapers and magazines in Vietnam are written in the quoc ngu *system. It uses the same alphabet as English, but it has many accents.*

Going to school

The people of Vietnam value education and learning. Nine out of ten Vietnamese can read and write. Schools are free, and run by the government. Vietnamese students are eager to learn, study hard, and respect their teachers.

The first years

Students aged six to eleven go to primary school, where they learn reading, writing, and arithmetic. Students are very respectful of their teachers and try hard in class. Rules are strongly enforced at school, and disobedient students are punished harshly by their teachers. Students do not receive letter or number grades. Instead, parents are sent notes from the school each month, telling them where their child ranks in the class.

Few supplies

With so many children to educate and so little money, schools often cannot afford supplies. Some classrooms have little more than old wooden benches, scratched tables, and one teacher for 50 students. Children go to school six days a week. Many must walk a long distance from their home to their school.

A school day

Students often go to class in shifts so that all the children in a community can attend school. One group of students goes to school early in the morning, from 7:30 to 11:30. A second group goes to school in the afternoon. Often there is a long break for lunch when the weather gets very hot. People often take a nap after lunch.

Higher education

After elementary school, many children leave school and start working to earn a wage. Some students, however, go to secondary school where they learn history, geography, science, and English. To get into secondary school, the students must pass difficult exams. After secondary school they can go to university or a vocational school that provides special training for trades such as mechanics, carpentry, or agriculture. Many students hope to go to university so they will be able to get a well-paying job in the city.

(above) In many schools, students wear a uniform consisting of a white shirt and red scarf.

Thu's day

It is still dark outside when ten-year-old Thu's mother calls softly to wake her up at five a.m. It is time for Thu to help her grandmother and mother clean and chop vegetables for the small food stand they operate at the market. Thu's father is already at work. He drives a cyclo.

As the sun begins to shine through the windows, Mother and Grandmother leave for the market. Thu changes into her school uniform and puts her books and homework into her schoolbag. After leaving the apartment, Thu squeezes her way along the crowded streets towards school.

Before her classes start, she sits and talks with her friends in the hallway. Everyone is excited and nervous to find out how they did on yesterday's math test. To her delight, Thu learns that she scored third in her class!

In the afternoon, the students go on their annual field trip. This year it is to the city zoo. The teacher points out **endangered** animals from Vietnam's wilderness, such as tigers, elephants, and the Javan rhinoceros. Thu's favorite animals are the lively monkeys.

At the end of the school day, Thu walks home through the market, stopping to visit Mother's food stall and have a drink of coconut milk. Grandmother is tired, so she joins Thu on the walk home.

In the evening, Mother and Father return home. Thu and Grandmother have prepared a dinner of stir-fried vegetables and tofu, which they eat over a heap of rice noodles. Everyone is proud to hear that Thu had a high score on her math test. The family drinks a pot of hot tea as they chat before going to bed.

(above) While waiting for class to begin, Thu and her classmates discuss yesterday's math test.

Making a living

Many years of war and an unstable economy have made life difficult for the Vietnamese people. Many people are unemployed or **underemployed**. Those who work often do not earn enough money to support themselves and their family. Some must take on second jobs.

Farm work

Most Vietnamese people are farm workers. Rice is the biggest crop grown. Rice fields make up about 75 percent of all farmland. The fertile land allows farmers to grow a wide variety of other foods, such as corn, potatoes, sugar cane, sweet potatoes, tomatoes, snow peas, beans, cabbage, bananas and other fruit. **Cash crops** such as rubber, tea, tobacco, peanuts, pepper, and coffee are also grown. More than half the farmers in Vietnam are women.

Private business

Vietnam is a communist country. In communist countries, the government owns industries and businesses. Factory workers, miners, teachers, and scientists are all government employees. Recently, the government has allowed people to set up their own businesses because of a policy called *doi moi*, or "new thinking." Foreign companies are opening offices and factories in Vietnam. Young people want to work for foreign companies because they usually pay well. The government has also given more freedom to farmers. The government, however, still has strict control over most businesses.

(below) These workers are harvesting tea. Vietnam sells a lot of its tea to other countries.

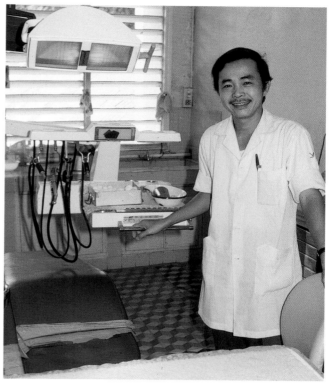

(left) Many people set up stalls on the street and offer all kinds of services. These men operate their own shoe repair business.

(below) Since doi moi, many professionals such as dentists and doctors have set up their own offices in larger cities. They can earn more money there than they can by working in hospitals.

Artisans

Many people are **artisans**. They earn their living by selling their crafts. Traditional crafts include woodcarving, embroidery, silk painting, weaving, and lacquerware. Lacquerware items, made from wood, are beautifully painted and then covered with a hard, shiny coating.

Industry

Rice, oil, gas, coffee, rubber, and garments are Vietnam's most important sources of income, or money. The country is struggling to develop other industries to support its people. Tourism has also become an important industry.

Merchants

Many people operate small businesses at a local market. Prices are negotiated through friendly bargaining. The buyer suggests a low price, and the seller tries to insist on a higher one. In the end, the buyer and seller agree on a price—usually something in between. In the villages, people usually sell what they have grown or made. In cities, people often sell products that have been manufactured or imported. There are few department stores, so people rely on the markets to buy many of the things they need.

(right) Merchants sell all kinds of goods, such as food, clothing, household items, and crafts at Vietnam's many markets.

 # Sports and leisure

Many people work six days a week, from sunrise to sunset. They do not have a lot of free time, but they participate in sports and other activities as a way of socializing with others and keeping fit. There are community centers and clubs where people can play sports. Many people simply organize their own small games for friendly competition. Students learn to play sports in school during gym class.

Sports

Gymnastics, badminton, table tennis, swimming, cycling, tennis, and volleyball are popular sports in Vietnam. Almost everyone owns a bicycle. Many people stay fit just by pedaling to work! Soccer is Vietnam's most popular sport. People play friendly games of soccer and also cheer for their favorite local, semi-professional teams.

Martial arts

Martial arts have been practiced in Vietnam for hundreds of years. The Vietnamese style of martial arts is called *Viet Vo Dao*, which means "the martial way of the Viets." Today, Vietnam is known around the world for its martial arts schools. Students practice tae kwon do, *wushu*, judo, karate, and kung fu. Martial arts are often a part of daily life in Vietnam. People of all ages meet in city parks to perform *tai chi* exercises before they start their work or school day.

(above) A group of women practice a form of tai chi in Cong Vien Van Hoa Park, Ho Chi Minh City. The long sticks represent swords.

Time to relax

Many Vietnamese prefer to spend leisure time visiting with family and friends. In villages, people often play bamboo flutes or share a game of cards or chess. Some village people save their money for a trip to the beach or a historic site. City workers who live close to the beach often go there to relax and cool off in the late afternoon. Some people in the city attend concerts or plays. An evening's entertainment, however, is often as simple as watching television or pulling up a chair to one of the many street stalls that sell food and drink.

Café life

After work in the cities—and in villages that have electricity—people gather with friends at local cafés. They chat with one another, play cards, and shoot pool. Young people enjoy visiting the *cafe kem*—the ice-cream café. Another place to spend an evening is the café video, where customers watch movies and television. In the cities, karaoke lounges are popular. People sing along to songs with words that appear on a video screen.

(above) Playing board games is a popular way for both young and old to pass a hot afternoon.

(below) The grounds of an ancient fort called the Citadel in the city of Hué provide an excellent spot for a friendly game of soccer.

Glossary

ancestor A person from whom one is descended

artisan A person skilled in a craft

bamboo A grassy plant with woody stems used to make items such as furniture, musical instruments, and houses

Buddhist A follower of the Buddhist religion, which is based on the teachings of the Buddha

cash crop A crop grown mainly for export

climate The usual weather conditions of a particular place, including temperature, rainfall, and humidity

Coa Dai A religion founded in Vietnam that accepts the teachings of many religious leaders

colony A land or people ruled by another country

culture The customs, beliefs, and arts of a group of people

dialect A way of speaking that differs from the standard form of the language in its words, sayings, and pronunciations

disowned Describing a person who is no longer accepted by his or her family

endangered Describing a plant or animal species that could soon become extinct

ethnic minority An ethnic group that lives in an area where a larger number of people belong to other ethnic groups

generation A group of people born within twenty years of one another. Grandparents, parents and children make up three generations

hatchery A place where eggs are hatched

incense A substance that produces a sweet-smelling smoke when burned

land mine A bomb that is buried in the ground and explodes when someone walks or drives over it

martial arts A sport that uses the techniques of fighting and self-defense, which were once part of hand-to-hand battle

missionary A person who travels to a foreign country to spread a particular religion

rural Relating to the countryside

shrine A special place that is reserved for the worship of something sacred; a place where sacred things are kept

traditional Describing customs that are handed down from one generation to another

tributary A river that flows into a larger body of water

underemployed Describing a person who has a job but does not earn enough money to support him or herself

Index

1 2 3 4 5 6 7 8 9 0   Printed in the USA   0 9 8 7 6 5 4 3 2 1